T0107413

THE *Transformations* COLLECTION

DONNA P. CHAMBERS

This book is a work of non-fiction. Unless otherwise noted, the author and the publisher make no explicit guarantees as to the accuracy of the information contained in this book and in some cases, names of people and places have been altered to protect their privacy.

WestBow Press books may be ordered through booksellers or by contacting:

WestBow Press
A Division of Thomas Nelson & Zondervan
1663 Liberty Drive
Bloomington, IN 47403
www.westbowpress.com
844-714-3454

ISBN: 979-8-3850-0604-5 (sc)
ISBN: 979-8-3850-0605-2 (e)

Library of Congress Control Number: 2023916061

Print information available on the last page.

WestBow Press rev. date: 11/13/2023

CONTENTS

THE GOOD HAIR DAY

It was one of those days where I hoped everything would be just right. I was scheduled to teach a new training class at work. Because of a lack of self-confidence in my presentation skills, I was not looking forward to it. I would much rather write the procedures, which doing so was part of my primary job function but had been asked to fill in for the regular trainer who was on vacation.

To help boost my self-assurance, I wore an outfit that looked sophisticated, yet was very comfortable. I also chose a hair style that I was well accustomed to and felt secure in. The skirt had a paisley pattern splashed with deep blues and purples trimmed with a soft beige color. The blouse matched the beige of the trim and was enhanced by a vest that went beautifully with the blue in the skirt. Leaving the back of my hair long and flowing, I pulled the top and sides into a respectable looking barrette and felt ready to face the day.

Halfway through the morning, I began to relax. I

felt like the week wasn't going to be so bad after all. I had a great group of trainees to work with who seemed to understand the material well, even though it was a lot to grasp in the short time frame allotted. Before I knew it, we were ready to break for lunch.

After giving the trainees directions to the various eating establishments in the area, I decided I would grab something quick to bring back to my desk to eat. I headed down to the little deli in the lobby. As I approached the entrance, I turned my head slightly to the right to look at the menu that was displayed out front. It seemed there was something different about the menu that day, but I could not put my finger on what it was. It was in the same place as usual, had a list of entrees giving their description and prices, as expected, and customarily announced the soup for the day. So, what was it that was different? Suddenly, without warning, it hit me, or should I say I hit it!

Somewhere within that lobby, I heard a noise that I can only describe as a dull "thud" combined with a slight "ping"! I felt a lump rise in my throat, and on my forehead, as I realized the sound had come from much closer than I ever wanted to imagine.

When you have a little deli with glass walls and glass doors, inside the lobby of a much larger building, you can prop your door open and situate your menu neatly behind it. All your customers can then look through the glass and read the menu as they approach. They do not have to worry about struggling with an awkward door on their way in and, even better, on their way out when their hands are full.

So, who had the bright idea to close the door that day, anyway? Do they not know that their patrons have acquired a sense of security and well-being just knowing the door is always open for them? Well, at least one has!

Since it was the busiest time of the day, only a million people were inside to witness the blunder. Although each of their faces had become a complete blur to me, I was appalled at the possibility that even one could be from my new training class. Therefore, I felt it necessary to explain to the group after lunch, reliving the agony, the reason their instructor walked right into a closed, glass door!

In reflecting back, I wonder how many other "doors" in my life do I assume will always be open? I sometimes pay no attention to where I am going. I put forth no effort to reach out and "grab the handle" to open a door that may be closing for me or already closed. Setting aside time to spend uninterrupted with my spouse, children or grandchildren, continuing my education, accepting a better job offer, nurturing an important friendship, finding time to write, or making things right with my gracious Creator, are just a few examples that come to mind.

Unfortunately, I do not remember much else about that training class, except a comment one of the trainees wrote when evaluating me at the end of the week; "She has nice hair." So maybe I did something right that day!

THE TRANSFORMATIONS

When I was sixteen years old, I watched my younger brother's life slowly slip away in pain and suffering because of cancer. He was only ten months younger than me, but at the age of fifteen had gone through more than most people will ever go through in their entire lives. He lost his leg due to the disease which had settled in his bone. Later it gripped his chest causing a lung to collapse and his heart to push over to the other side from the tumors. Within a total of eight short months the sickness completed its ultimate purpose: death. I can only describe my feelings when he died as numb and removed from the reality of the situation. I felt so incredibly alone. How could life be so cruel, short, and fragile? At least this life as we know it. Later, it would be his death that played a major role in my total transformation. The set of values and standards that I have adopted since that time have carried me through the major events, both good and bad of my life, and continue to lead me through to this present day.

Our family was in no way religious, nor did we engage in any type of religious practices such as prayer or Bible reading. We had attended church when my brother and I were at a preschool age but had stopped by the time we were in school. Our father, who had no objections to the thought of there being a God who created us all, had a deep dislike for organized religions, which he was very vocal about. Being a child and not really understanding his objections, I developed a tainted view of my own toward anything resembling religion, the Bible and Christian people. I believe now this was part of the reason I became plagued with feelings of hopelessness, purposelessness, and fear. These feelings were only magnified by the unnecessary suffering and death of my little brother. I began to experiment with drugs and alcohol, developed a heavy cigarette smoking habit and adopted an overall bad attitude towards life.

Shortly after my brother passed away, I became another statistic of the 70's: A high-school drop-out and a pregnant, unwed seventeen-year-old on public assistance, called 'welfare' back then to most.

Life was dark. My heart was dark. But it was during that darkness that I heard a message that began to penetrate my confused mind and hardened heart. My parents had divorced right before my brother had gotten sick and my mom became one of the "others." I thought she was totally ruined and would tell anyone who would give me an ear that she was wacky. But she and her friends kept sharing with me the message that God loved me, just the way I was, dark heart, bad attitude, and all, and that His son, Jesus, died for me! Well, this certainly was new! And my mom was different, like a brand-new person. "Is it possible that God is real, and he is personally interested in me and my life?", I began to ask myself.

It is hard to describe the change that began to take hold of my heart and life as I realized it was all true. God ***is*** real, and he ***is*** personally interested in my life. He gave his Son for me, and his Son gave his life for me! So that was what my brother had experienced exactly one week before he died! That was why he tried to tell the nurses and others around him to give their hearts and lives to Christ. That explains the glow I saw on his face, despite the pain I knew he was in, the night we said good-bye to each other for the last time. That explains the vision I saw of him walking (in what looked like a desert, yet it was not hot or dry) with Jesus! And my brother had both of his legs! There were other children with them, who, along with my brother, would jump and skip around Jesus every few steps, laughing and having true fun. With the vision also came the knowledge that amid the fun, Jesus was answering all their questions about life and was sharing some deep, eternal truths that we here on earth are not privileged to yet know.

Early in 1977, I asked Jesus Christ to come into my heart and life and have not been the same since. I no longer experiment with drugs or alcohol and have not smoked a cigarette since that date. My son's father and I were married shortly after he was born, and we now share a wonderful life together.

Our son is now almost thirty-nine years old. He spent ten years serving our country in the Navy, traveling everywhere from Greece (where he was mistaken for one of the Backstreet Boys, being followed around by folks asking for his autograph!) to Bahrain. With two incredible sons of his own, and now part of a blended family with a precious wife with three awesome children of her own, he has become quite the family man!

We have two beautiful daughters, both with families of their own. Our oldest daughter has two rambunctious sons who are as different from each other in personality as night is from day. I could fill a book with some of the cute things they say – hmm, maybe I will! (Note to self: be sure to share in a story someday the miracle of how God saved the oldest one's life the day after he was born and the youngest one's understanding of 'rolling dice'!).

Our youngest daughter gave us our first granddaughter, who has as fiery a personality as her momma. As cute as a button, she is showered with love and affection and the sharpest outfits you can imagine, with momma making a lot of them herself! At two years of age, she had already learned to layer tank tops over dresses with pants underneath. So stylish!

While we still struggled at times financially, we were finally able to get off public assistance. My husband started his own house painting business, and I went back to school and earned my high-school diploma. I was then able to get a job with a credit card company, doing everything from printing copies of statements from micro-fiche to programming our call center application. I am now working as a Data Architect designing databases.

But more important than all my and my family's accomplishments over the years, is the new heart I have been given in Christ and my new attitude toward life! Life is no longer dark. And my heart is bright with the light of Christ's love.

And best of all: I know I will see Bobby again when this life is over. We will run, jump, and laugh together in that beautiful place with the One who transformed my heart and mind here on this earth and his forever in eternity!

'...What counts is whether we have been transformed into a new creation.' Galatians 6:15 (NLT)

'But let me reveal to you a wonderful secret. We will not all die, but we will all be transformed!' I Corinthians 15:51 (NLT)

'This means that anyone who belongs to Christ has become a new person. The old life is gone; a new life has begun.' II Corinthians 5:17 (NLT)

Authors reflection

In my earliest years as a Christian, a scripture that spoke strongly to me was I Thessalonians 4: 11-12. Here is how it reads in the NLT 1996 version: 'This should be your ambition: to live a quiet life, minding your own business and working with your hands, just as we commanded you before. As a result, people who are not Christians will respect the way you live, and you will not need to depend on others ***to meet your financial needs.***' (emphasis mine). This has become one of my 'Life Scriptures'. It encouraged me that, for our family, we needed to become financially independent and off public assistance. I am in no way saying to anyone that it is wrong to be ***on*** public assistance. We certainly needed it at the time.

I am also ***not*** putting down anyone who struggles with drugs, alcohol or smoking. God takes each of us on our own personal journey and works everything out for our good and His glory. He gives the strength needed to overcome any struggles that may be controlling our lives – 'hurts, hang-ups, or habits' as described in a program I was a part of called 'Celebrate Recovery'.

My original story was written in 2006 when grandson #3 was first born to our oldest daughter.

I then updated this version in 2014 with our family changes up to that point, which included grandson #4, our first granddaughter, and three more grandchildren by marriage. We later welcomed another granddaughter and two great grandsons.

I have come to realize that since this is my own personal testimony, it could literally be updated every year!

My prayer in sharing my story is so you can see how God can transform a life heading in one direction - full of fear, depression and darkness - and turn it around in a completely new direction – His direction - full of peace and joy and light! I pray that it will point you, the precious reader, to the only true hope for the world and for your own life: Jesus Christ. Without Him there is no hope but with Him we ALL have not only hope but salvation and a new life!

THE ARRIVAL

Bob knew today was going to be special. He had waited for what seemed an eternity for it to come. He checked all the last-minute arrangements. He sent out reminders to those he knew needed to be there. The decorations and food were ready. The pianist was ready to play that one special song that meant so much.

Bob's mother was coming in on the first flight, and everything was ready for her arrival.

Oh, how he had longed over the years to be able to sit with her on the terrace of his new home, soaking in the warmth, talking, and laughing with her over a hot cup of coffee about her life. So many trials and tragedies she had gone through, yet was always full of life, love, forgiveness and that stubborn, never give up type of faith that is so rare in the world these days.

He remembered when he went through the worst trial in his own life, she was right there beside him. He longed to talk with her and thank her for everything she had done and somehow do something stellar to show his deep gratitude. Maybe this gathering would be it.

Finally, at 1:32 pm the announcement heralded through the air that flight 101707 had arrived!

Donna was exhausted. She had been back and forth for the last few weeks between her house and the hospital doing everything she could to help her mother who'd had a third stroke. This one left Ruth unable to eat, drink or barely even breathe on her own. The family agonized over whether to pull her off the feeding tube, but the day came when that decision had to be made.

Donna's stepfather, John, remembered how his own mother had lingered on life support for years. To watch her lying in bed as a vegetable was heart wrenching. She had absolutely no quality of life, so he was determined that his beloved Ruth was not going to go through the same.

The decision was made. The feeding tube was removed, and Ruth was moved from the hospital back to the nursing home where she had resided the last year. But this time when Donna went to visit, things were different. Before, Donna was greeted with a bright happy smile. Sometimes there was even recognition in those soft brown eyes. But now, everything was quiet, lifeless, and downright eerie.

There they sat for the next several days. Waiting. Agonizing. Haunted with the thought that maybe they had not done the right thing.

They did everything they could to make Ruth as comfortable as possible, administering pain medication as needed. Donna still hung on to the hope that her mother might somehow miraculously pull through.

Ruth had loved playing the piano, so Donna brought a player and CD of piano songs that included her mother's favorites. But in the chaos of trying to make that dreaded decision with John, she had left it at John's house.

Today when Donna arrived at the nursing home, Ruth was fidgety and agitated. She was restless and seemed frightened. Usually, John was there well before Donna, but it was nearly noon, and he was nowhere in sight. Maybe Ruth sensed his absence and that's what had her so upset. But Donna had an idea. If she could catch John before he headed out, she could have him grab the CD player and music. She called and sure enough, he was just about to leave the house and grabbed it on his way out.

As soon as John arrived, Donna plugged the player in and popped in the CD. Ruth's reaction was instant. She stopped fidgeting. A peacefulness settled over her that was uncanny and hard to describe or comprehend.

Donna knew deep down in her heart that this was it. She stood on one side of the bed and stroked Ruth's hair, talking softly to her, trying to let her know that she was there and loved her. John was on the other side of the bed, holding Ruth's hand and whispering encouragement into her ear as the melody to 'The Old Rugged Cross' filled the air.

Dareus and Cameron knew they had their job cut out for them. There was much darkness they needed to wade through to accomplish their mission. But they could feel the prayers of the saints giving them strength. After all, this was the best part of their job. They saw a light shining through the darkness and heard the sweet sound of a piano playing softly in the distance, getting louder and clearer as they approached.

As Ruth heard the soft tune of 'The Old Rugged Cross' playing somewhere nearby, she was overwhelmed with a sense of peace and well-being. She knew her daughter Donna was there, stroking her hair, and her beloved husband John was holding her hand. She heard John whisper softly to her, 'Go ahead, don't be afraid, just take Jesus's hand.' And that is exactly what she did.

Dareus and Cameron were overjoyed as they escorted her right into the arms of their Lord and hers, Jesus Christ, the Master Creator.

As the Master gently cupped Ruth's face in His hands, He wiped away all tears which came from the deep pain of her life and replaced them with tears of joy. She knew she would never feel pain or suffering again.

Although she was now far, far away from the place she had called home for 87 years, she could still hear 'The Old Rugged Cross' playing on the piano. But it was different. It was clearer than any music she had ever heard on earth. It seemed alive as the recalled words resonated in her soul like never before. She felt lavished in love, joy and peace that surpassed any human understanding.

She looked out over the terrace of the home where she found herself, to the stunning beauty surrounding it. She noticed what looked like a celebration taking place in the distance. Dareus and Cameron smiled at each other as they began to escort her towards it.

As they approached, she thought she recognized the person standing in front of the crowd. Yes, she did! It was her son Bob, who had died of cancer at just fifteen years of age. To add to her joy, although one of his legs had been amputated because of the dreadful disease, he was walking normally on both legs!

Her arrival was like nothing she had ever experienced. Bob, with pride, began to walk her through the crowd and watched with delight as she recognized her loved ones who had gone on before.

There was Theresa, her granddaughter who was abused and killed while just a baby. How happy Theresa was here! No scars, no bruises, no trace whatsoever of what had been done to her. And now, Ruth's memory of the person who did it was fading completely away.

And there, to the right of Theresa, was Ruth's baby brother Axel! He was still a baby but was walking, talking, laughing and jumping around Theresa playfully. On Earth, he had died at only 11 months of age when their mother, suffering from a severe post-partum depression, tried taking her own life but accidently took his in the process. Ruth would have died as well, had she been home, but she had just started school and was not there when the pilot light was blown out of the stove and the deadly gas filled the house.

But wait, was that Ruth's mother shyly standing behind Axel with a bright smile on her face? It was! Ruth remembered how her mother, after Axel's death, spent the remainder of her life in a mental institution. As soon as Ruth was old enough, she would visit faithfully every week. Ruth's mother could not speak a word of English, so Ruth brought a Swedish Bible in to her. How her mother's face lit up with recognition of the words! And those words did their work, because here Ruth's mother was, forgiven, saved and completely redeemed. What an arrival that one must have been!

The more people Ruth saw, the more joy she felt. She could no longer remember what pain and suffering felt like. She had arrived. She was home.

As Ruth slipped away from Donna and John, Donna heard John say, "Oh how I wish I was going with her". His words echoed in Ruth's mind as she was in that happy place, so she whispered back "Oh, you will be with me someday, my beloved. And I will wait in anticipation for the day of your arrival!"

Bob, with pride, escorted his mother up to the terrace of his home where hers could be seen in the distance. They enjoyed a hot cup of coffee together, laughing, talking and crying tears of joy, while soaking in the warmth of the Son who permeated every corner.

Authors reflection

My brother Bobby arrived in Heaven in the summer of 1974. He was only 15 years old.

When I was a very young girl, we used to pick up my grandmother from the mental institution each week and take her out for 'coffee' and 'ice cream' – the only 2 words I ever heard her say in English. My mom shared with us years later about the Swedish Bible and how her mother's eyes lit up when she was given it! My mother also shared the tragic story of how her mother ended up in the mental institution because of the attempted suicide and the accidental death of my mom's little brother.

All the other incidents in this story are true as I was either told them or experienced them firsthand. Each one is a whole story in and of itself that I hope to one day also put into writing. Although I am not 100% sure about some of the details, i.e., the age of Axel when he died, I took a guess based on the other pieces of information from my mom as she told the story.

Without a doubt, my mother was an incredible woman. She faced many trials and tragedies in her life that I hope to be able to write about someday. To note here a few, she went through a very painful divorce from my father, but soon after gave her heart to Jesus and became a new person in Christ! Unfortunately, tragedy struck again when my brother became ill and died of cancer. But being a new believer, she never gave up and literally prayed Bobby into the kingdom! Hardly ever leaving his side (sleeping in the hospital with him at night and then going to work from there during the day), she had the privilege of seeing and hearing him give his heart to the Lord exactly 1 week before he died! God is amazing!

In the fall of 2007, as I was getting ready one morning to take the trip back up to see my mom after her third stroke, a 'picture' dropped in my mind of my brother waiting at a sort of train station for her to arrive. That was when this story was born in my heart. What a blessing to finally have been able to get it from my heart onto the written page! I pray it inspires you to know that Heaven is truly real, and we have a blessed hope because of what Jesus did on the cross so that we could be forgiven for all our sins! Please don't hesitate to ask Jesus Christ into your heart if you have not done so already. You will never, ever regret it!

These are the words of Jesus to you: 'Don't let your hearts be troubled. Trust in God, and trust also in me. There is **more than enough room** (*emphasis mine*) in my father's home. If this were not so, would I have told you that I am going to prepare a place for you? **When everything is ready, I will come and get you** (*emphasis mine*), so that you will always be with me where I am' John 14:1-3 (NLT 2015).

Looking forward to that day!

NO ROOM

Matea loved everything about the barn. The smell of fresh hay. The feel of the soft earth under her bare feet. Hearing the coo of the pigeons, the cluck of the chickens, the bleat of the goats, the bray of the donkeys, and even the occasional squeak of a mouse scampering in the corner. The feel of the soft fur under her hands of those she was able to pet and love on. The animals were her friends. They loved her unconditionally. When things got rough, when she was bullied, when she was made fun of because she was too painfully shy to speak up in a crowd, when there was absolutely no room for her to play with the other children in their games, she would run home and find complete solace in the barn.

When she was very young, she would clean out the animal trough and fill it with straw, wrapping her doll baby with strips of cloth meant for wrapping newborn animals so they wouldn't thrash around while being inspected for spots or blemishes. She would lay her baby in the trough and sing it sweetly to sleep with her animal friends gathered around listening in with a hush. Mama had to practically drag her out when it was time for the evening meal and complained that she was starting to smell just like a donkey! Matea didn't care. She felt safe in the barn. She felt at peace in the barn. She felt hidden under the very wings of God in the barn.

But now, as she was getting older, it became harder to find the time to spend in her favorite place. She often gave thanks to God that her morning chores involved gathering the fresh eggs laid by the chickens, milking the goats and brushing down the donkeys. Otherwise, she would never get to see or hear them or breathe in the deep smells she had grown to love. Between her sewing and cooking lessons and the household chores needing to be done inside, her times of solace in the barn were few and far between.

On Matea's 16th birthday, Mama and Papa announced two things that left Matea staring at them in stunned silence. The first: the family had scrimped and saved and would be able to purchase a lamb for this year's sacrifice. A lamb? It was hard enough to take care of the pigeons knowing that their only purpose was to be sacrificed as an offering and atonement for the sins of the family. But now a lamb? Before her parents got their second announcement out, she had already begun to plot how she would make that lamb's life the best any lamb could ever have before it was slaughtered. Her mind raced to some of the nearest springs she could take him to for watering, and some of the freshest, greenest grass for his nourishment and comfort while resting.

Then came the bombshell of all bombshells: Matea was to be married off by the end of the year. She knew this day would come. It happened to all the girls her age, but the reality of it happening to her had just about taken her breath away. Who was it? What kind of a man would he be? How would he treat her? Would she grow to somehow love him? The questions swirled in her mind like rapids in a wild running river.

Their choice was the wood worker who lived two towns over. Matea racked her brain to try and place him. Her parents helped jog her memory by relaying the few times she had been with them when they went to his shop to purchase some furnishings. They assured her he was a good and godly man who would take very good care of her. Their hearts were at peace with their choice, and they prayed hers would be as well.

As the realization of who it was finally sunk in, Matea knew in her heart she should be grateful. Although he was much older than she, he seemed a kind enough man in the few encounters she had had with him. And was that her heart skipping a beat as she remembered the time most recent when he had flashed his gentle smile her way?

As soon as Mama and Papa were done with their announcements, Matea went to the only place where she could cry to her heart's content and know she would be accepted, loved and not criticized. The barn. But this time, her time there was a bit different. She had an encounter that would change her life forever.

Although it was less than nine months since Matea had a chance to spend time with her beloved animals in the barn, it felt like a lifetime. The day her parents announced her marriage was the last time she had been able to drink in the smell of the fresh straw and feel the earth's dampness underneath her feet. Now that she was betrothed to the woodworker a few towns over, her life was in a whirlwind. She had become pregnant before they were married and felt the heavy judgment and condemnation thrown her way by both her family and those, she thought were her friends. It was so hard to see the hurt and grief in Mama and Papa's eyes. She tried to explain but the words came out in a jumble every time.

How grateful Matea was that her betrothed had determined not to humiliate her publicly. His plan was to call off the marriage privately, but then, to Matea's amazement, after a visit from an angel in a dream, he decided to marry her after all. Matea could not help but wonder if he would one day regret his decision.

Toward the end of Matea's pregnancy, the news came through that her fiancé would need to travel all the way to Bethlehem because of a census he was required to register in. To Matea's relief he did not hesitate to take her with him. Although she knew the travel would be rough, anything was better than facing alone the glaring looks she received from so many of the town's folk. While her family had begun to believe her innocence in the pregnancy, there were still many who treated her as an outcast.

The traveling was even tougher than Matea had anticipated. With her being so heavy with child, it took twice as long to reach their destination than the other families traveling the same distance. And the nagging pain she felt in her back seemed to be from more than just the travel. She found herself longing for a nice cool bath and a soft bed to lie on.

Finally reaching their destination they headed straight to their relatives as planned. Unfortunately, with so many other relatives traveling to the same destination, and since they were so late, they were informed the house was full and they would need to find some public lodging.

After going to several different establishments, it was getting late, and Matea's pain was increasing greatly. She began to wonder for the first time if God's plan was for her to have His child while riding on the back of a donkey!

At the last place they tried it seemed a lifetime before the door was answered. The innkeeper quickly sized up their situation and with pity in his heart advised the only place he had that they could at least lay their heads down was in the barn behind the property.

Before Joseph could answer one way or another, Mary boldly shouted to the innkeeper from atop the donkey, "We'll take it!" Joseph looked at her in disbelief. He was ready to fight for a better place! "Matea", he replied.

It had been such a long time since Joseph called her by her childhood nickname. When they were first betrothed, he called her Metea all the time. It was the nickname given to her by her mother after an extremely rough pregnancy. Although, when their miracle was born, they officially gave her the name Mary because of the tradition of passing down family names, to her mother, and then later to Joseph, she was Metea, 'God's gift'. Once Mary became pregnant, and even though Joseph knew the child she carried was from God, she still felt things would always be a bit strained between them. But now, with that one word, Mary knew all was well. He still thought of her as God's gift to him!

"I want a good, comfortable, peaceful and safe place for you to have God's child", Joseph continued.

"Oh Joseph, you are such a kind and good man. My heart bursts with love for you! But please know, there is no place more peaceful nor safe that we can go for me to have God's child. I know just what to do. I am at home in the barn."

So, Mary pondered in her heart the miracle of the place God had provided for them.

"She gave birth to her firstborn son. She wrapped him snugly in strips of cloth and laid him in a manger, because there was no lodging available for them". (Luke 2:7 NLT)

And years later she had the privilege of hearing her son, God's Son, say, "Don't let your hearts be troubled. Trust in God, and trust also in me. There is **more than enough room** (*emphasis mine*) in my Father's home. If this were not so, would I have told you that I am going to prepare a place for you? When everything is ready, I will come and get you, so that you will always be with me where I am" John 14:1-3 (NLT 2015).

Authors reflection

This story was born out of the testimony of how God always, always knows exactly what I need when I am struggling with some hurt or difficult circumstance beyond my control. He provides 'apples of gold' which meet the deepest cries of my heart in a way that only He could know.

He reminds me over and over how deeply He loves me (Daniel 10:19 NLT: 'Don't be afraid', he said, 'for you are deeply loved by God. Be at peace; take heart and be strong!'). He has promised in Isaiah 46:4 (NLT) 'I will be your God throughout your lifetime – until your hair is white with age. I made you, and I will care for you. I will carry you along and save you.'

I was going through one of those extremely difficult times and thought of Mary. What if her child being born in a barn was really a blessing from God for ***her***? What if it helped her know just how much He personally cared about her and loved her? What if the very provision of that humble place met some deep need in ***her*** heart?

It would be just like God to do that!!

My disclaimer is that this is purely fictional except the scripture reference where she wrapped Jesus snugly in strips of cloth and laid Him in a manger, and Jesus's words in John 14:1-3. Although I did some very brief research (see below regarding the name Matea) I make no claim to have all the facts straight, nor have I scholarly woven in Biblical truths. This is purely from a 'what if' perspective. I pray you enjoyed reading it as much as I enjoyed writing it!

From charlies-names.com when Googling '**What does the name Matea mean?**'

Matea means "gift of Yahweh" or "gift of God" (from Hebrew "mattath/מַתָּת" = gift + "yah/יָה" = referring to the Hebrew God).

LEAN IN LIKE A DOG

My husband and I brought our new chocolate Labrador Retriever home on New Year's Day. The middle of winter New Year's Day. She was the first dog either one of us had ever had - ever. Why we picked a chocolate lab for our first dog, I'll never know. Hadn't we ever seen the movie 'Marley And Me'? Yes, but never having a dog meant the movie was just that – a movie, a fantasy. It wasn't until after we already had her that I read how chocolates are usually the most boisterous and energetic of the breed. Shouldn't we have done some research before we brought her home? That would have made way too much sense!

House training Molly in the middle of winter was brutal. At times, with tears streaming down my face I would say, "I. Cannot. Do. This." And why hadn't anyone told me about puppy piranha-like teeth? I could have worn armor for protection!

She eventually calmed down and we fell absolutely in love with her. It's striking how completely she trusts us to meet all her needs. She does this thing where she will lean her now 75-pound body into our legs. Our reaction of course is to lavish her with love and affection in return.

In reflecting how Jesus uses nature in many of his teachings, the story in Matthew chapter 15 struck a special chord in my soul (quotes taken from the NLT 2015 version). A Gentile woman was asking Jesus to heal her daughter. He responded, "I was sent only to help God's lost sheep – the people of Israel" (from vs. 24), but she kept coming pleading with him to help her. Finally, he said, "It isn't right to take food from the children and throw it to the dogs." (from vs. 26)

Woah! There is a whole list of ways she could have reacted to that one: "Oh no you didn't!" comes to mind.

But this amazing woman's heart and mind were not on the things of this world. Her response was draped in love for her daughter and in the realm of eternity, not what anyone around her thought or how her pride may or may not have been hurt. Her response was filled with the humble respect, love, and trust she had for Jesus. "That's true Lord, but even the dogs are allowed to eat the scraps that fall beneath their master's table." (from vs. 27)

And His final answer: ""Dear woman," Jesus said to her, "your faith is great. Your request is granted." And her daughter was instantly healed." (vs. 28) Wow!

May God help us to react with such love, respect, and trust in our Savior. May we recognize the amazing grace of the Lamb of God who was slain for the world and lean into His love like a trusting dog leans into its master. And let Him lavish His love and goodness back on us. Psalm 31:19 (NLT) says, "How great is the goodness you have stored up for those who fear you. You lavish it on those who come to you for protection, blessing them before the watching world."

How is Molly doing today? I answer the same way I do when anyone asks me. She. Is. Perfect!

WHEN GOD ANSWERS PRAYERS THAT HURT

Shortly after I had given my heart and life to Christ, my older sister, who had become a Christian a few years before me, became caught up again in her old lifestyle of drinking and drugging.

Our lives went in completely opposite directions with no real relationship with each other until about 7 years ago.

Her husband, who was an incredibly stable force in her life, had just died from a short but deadly illness. She found out within weeks of his passing that she had cancer.

I had just taken an early retirement and was on my way to becoming an accomplished (and famous!) best-selling author. Or travel the world as a speaker at women's conferences. Or take up art again and paint my way to stardom. The possibilities were endless!

But then I got the call. It was one of my sister's 'friends' asking for help.

During the dark days ahead, God used me to literally save my sisters life from a drug overdose and get her temporarily into an assisted living facility where they controlled her pain medications. With His continued grace and strength, I basically put my life on hold to take her for her psychiatrist and medical doctor appointments as well as chemo treatments every week.

Because of her limited income, she was not able to have full residency at the facility and had about 60 days total to find another place within her means.

After an exhausting search, we finally found a place that she could afford. We filled out all the forms, met with the director, had a nice lunch, took the tour, and agreed on a date. She seemed to really like it and they seemed to like her. They knew she was a smoker and had agreed on a plan to allow her time and a designated place on the property she could do so.

But about a week before the move, my sister called to declare, "Donna, I'm staying here, and I am not moving!" I tried hard, in a kind way, to explain that was just not possible or practical. She could not afford it. But she was adamite! "I have prayed, and everyone here is praying with me that I can stay. God is going to answer our prayers. He will make a way!"

After our call, I can remember how hard it was for me to think that God would answer her prayer, because that answer to her prayer would cost me greatly. I had already poured thousands of dollars into helping her stay for the 60-day respite. I had already spent even thousands more on the enormous amounts of repair work that needed to be done on her home for it to sell. The only way she could stay is if I submitted my own financial information as a back-up/co-signer. I would have to use my retirement funds as collateral. How could I give even more than I already had? Would God answer her prayer? How could He?

The day had arrived for her to move. I called to check on her and, though she was sad, she was all packed and ready to go. As I left to pick her up, I received a call - in my car - from the new facility saying they had decided not to take her because she was a smoker and their district office decided not to allow it. I was devastated. I did not understand. Why would God answer a prayer that hurt me so drastically?

Proverbs 3:5-6 (NLT) says: "Trust in the Lord with all your heart, do not depend on your own understanding. Seek His will in all you do, and He will show you which path to take."

Could I do that in this situation? Could I trust that

God knows what is best for both me and my sister when it all seemed to hurt ***me*** so much?

With no other options available, I submitted my own financial information, became her co-signer, and wondered "What. Was. God. Doing?"

The answer became clear the first time she had to leave the facility a short time for medical reasons.

When I brought her back from a stay at the hospital, the aides and nurses shared with me that after a day or two without her, nearly all the residents made their way down to the lobby to inquire about Miss Chrissy!

Residents with canes, others with walkers, and even one dear soul who made her way around the facility in a motorized wheelchair, all congregated together at the front desk. The receptionist had to call the aides and nurses down who assured everyone "Miss Chrissy is fine! She is with her sister (whom by now they all knew and trusted) and will be back real soon. Please go back to your activities!"

You see, after a few weeks from entering the facility, once she was physically able, Chrissy was put on the welcoming committee. Her outgoing personality captured the hearts of the residents, nurses, aides and even the director. She prayed for anyone who wanted prayer and some of those who did not. Yes, she still struggled with her smoking habit, but what a far cry from overdosing on pain medication.

One of the aides summed it up nicely when she declared, "Miss Chrissy is the light of this place!"

Ahh… there it was… God. Is. Sovereign!

We found out that her friend who had originally called me, tragically died from a drug overdose about a year later. Had I not stepped in when I did; I have no doubt my sister would have died along side of her.

Me? I had to eventually go back to work to help make ends meet. My dreams were put on hold for a little while longer. But I am trusting "...that God causes everything to work together for the good of those who love God and are called according to His purpose for them." Romans 8:28 (NLT).

And I pray for God's grace and strength to embrace His answers to prayer in the future, even when they hurt.

Authors reflection (2023)

After 7 years of being at the facility, in the late summer of 2022, my sister began to decline significantly in her health, so Hospice was called in to keep her as comfortable as possible.

During those last few months, one of the residents would visit Chrissy every week, bringing her a cheerful card or small gift to help lift her spirit. I would read the following out loud to my sister from one of those cards, which perked her up every time.

The card title was "It's nice to know you", with "Thank you for being a friend!" on the inside.

The handwritten portion included:

"When I first arrived here, you warmly welcomed me and each day when I walked by you greeted me and made me feel like I was accepted…You probably don't realize how much it has meant to me. Today I read "Pain teaches God's love." You must be overflowing with his warm embrace...".

What a confirmation after all those years of God's complete sovereignty regarding my sister and the purpose for her last years on this earth!

PHOTO GALLERY

THE GOOD HAIR DAY

"Leaving the back of my hair long and flowing, I pulled the top and sides into a respectable looking barrette and felt ready to face the day."

THE TRANSFORMATIONS

Bobby and I together as babies

Our family in the early 60's. From left to right:
Me, Chris, Mom, Dad, and Bobby

Bobby and I working as a team hanging laundry.

Bobby at different ages.

Bobby shortly before his 'Heaven Birthday'.

Notice in the background on the lower left is a picture of me. Then, in the upper right is a picture of Chris when she was young. Although it is hard to see, in the lower right is a picture of Jesus kneeling in the Garden of Gethsemane. This was not planned when I took this picture all those years ago, but God had a plan. How appropriate for sharing these stories!

THE ARRIVAL

My mom in her younger years before she met my dad.

My mom with Bobby and me when we were babies.

Enjoying the snow? My Mom holding Bobby with Chris and me standing in the snow.

Chris, Mom and me after she'd had the 2nd of her 3 strokes.

Mom and John when they were first married.

Mom & John after a stroke. She used to say, "He takes such good care of me!"

Mom before her last stroke and her 'Heaven Birthday'.

LEAN IN LIKE A DOG

They start out so cute (not showing the 'piranha like' teeth)!!!

Molly becoming the perfect dog!

Molly now in her senior years.

WHEN GOD ANSWERS PRAYERS THAT HURT

My beautiful sister Chris.

Now if I could only get her to smile…

Here, let me show you. Say "Cheese".

Ah… there it is!!

MORE TRANSFORMATIONS
(Decades of Love)

Top left: Kirk and I in the 1980's; Top right: Kirk and I in the 1990's
Bottom: You know it's true love when he does something for
you he does ***NOT*** *want to do! Like riding a horse!*

Kirk and I in the 2000's. Celebrating nearly 50 years of marriage!

ABOUT THE AUTHOR

Donna's love for writing started as a young child after reading "The Forgotten Door" by Alexander Key. She remembers writing a story of her own shortly after but has no recollection of what it was about!

Since giving her heart to Christ at the age of 18, she now has unforgettable true (and sometimes painful) stories to write about from her life. Her prayer is that her stories point you, the precious reader, to the powerful transformative work that only God can do in a life through his one and only Son, Jesus the Christ.

Donna has been part of different choirs, worship teams, a lady's ensemble and the worship leader for a ministry called 'Celebrate Recovery' in her local church. She often marveled that people ***let*** her sing! She has taught Sunday School and Children's Church, held home Bible Studies and served on two different church boards.

She and her husband Kirk, married nearly 50 years, have 3 grown children, 9 grandchildren, 2 great grandchildren and a perfect chocolate lab named Molly. They love spending time with the entire crew whenever and wherever possible!